How Good Parents Raise Narcissistic Kids

(and What They Can Do About It)

"All rights reserved. This book or any portion thereof
may not be reproduced or used in any manner whatsoever
without the express written permission of the publisher
except for the use of brief quotations in a book review.
© 2020

Introduction

As a parent, you always try to look out for your kids and give them all the resources they need to do well in life; you endeavor to raise them in the best manner possible.

However, during this pursuit, we have some parents who, instead of guiding their kids, micromanage them, dominate them, emotionally abuse them, and may even seek validation from them.

If you haven't guessed it already, I am referring to narcissistic parents who may have good intentions, but somehow only end up sabotaging their child's self-esteem.

"How do I know of that?" You ask:

That's because I am a narcissistic mother, and now, when I look back at how I raised and treated my kids, I feel nothing but guilty for my behavior.

That said, I'm not the kind of person that would nurture remorse. I've learned a lot from my mistakes.

From these hard-learned lessons, I've gradually been able to better myself and my relationship with my kids.

I've also realized that there may be other narcissistic parents in the same boat I've been in for so long, many of whom may have young kids with tender minds that deserve nothing but love, care, and positive attention from parents.

Acknowledging that need, I decided to pen down this book as a means to guide and help all parents who may be knowingly or unknowingly ruling their kids and ruining their self-esteem, happiness, and emotional wellbeing in the process.

This book contains actionable information about how narcissism can destroy kids' lives. It also includes potent techniques you can use to remedy the problem, and a journal meant to help you analyze and record your behavior better so that you can bring about positive change in your life.

As you progress through this book and implement what you learn, you will slowly equip yourself with the tools you need to have to raise happy, healthy, and confident kids.

Without ado, let's kick-start this journey:

CHAPTER 1

When Good Parents Raise Narcissists Kids

Narcissism is *"a strong personality pattern governed by a grandiose sense of self-esteem, an intense lack of empathy for others, and a bad habit of constantly seeking approval and admiration."*

Narcissism is a standard development stage for most adolescents and young adults. To some extent, it's also part of being human; however, it becomes a serious problem to address if this personality trait takes over your entire personality.

If you are a narcissist, you believe you are the best at everything; thus, you feel entitled to superior treatment. Because of this belief, you may seek validation from everyone. You may also impose your needs on others. Besides that, you may be selectively oblivious to other peoples' rights. You may go as far as not showing an ounce of empathy for others —unless doing so shall help you get what you want.

One would think that narcissism is a behavior that someone would outgrow upon becoming a parent. Unfortunately, the many narcissistic parents who ruthlessly dominate their kids has proven otherwise:

How Narcissistic Parents Influence their Kids

Most narcissistic parents have gone through problems with their parents or have experienced deprivation at a level that turns them into being strangely controlling and emotionally cruel towards their kids.

Whatever the reason may be, the truth is that narcissistic parents don't offer their kids the positive, calm, happy, and nurturing environment all kids deserve. Instead of appreciating and loving their kids and being their support system, narcissistic parents expect that care and attention from their kids.

Children cannot offer continuous positive reinforcement that narcissists parents yearn for; neither do they always follow orders perfectly as dictated by their parents.

This discrepancy causes narcissistic parents to react negatively. Either they completely lose their interest in raising their kids and instead go searching for other sources from which to get validation and love, or they view their kids as their mirror reflection and become incredibly controlling towards them.

Before elaborating how narcissistic parents influence their kids, let us take a quick look at the prominent character traits of narcissists.

Use these traits to analyze your personality for these characteristics so that you can have a better idea of whether you're a narcissistic parent.

Character Traits of Narcissists

If you are a narcissist, you are likely to have many or all of the following characteristics:

- You have a grandiose sense of self-esteem.
- You think you are superior and better than your kids.

- You stay preoccupied with your fantasies revolving around immense brilliance, power, beauty, ideal love, or success.

- You believe you are special; that nobody can match your uniqueness.

- You have a sense of entitlement over everything.

- You constantly compare everyone against you, even your kids, and never seem to find any quality in even your progeny.

- You need extreme admiration from people, particularly your kids.

- You exhibit a very exploitative behavior towards people, including your children.

- You believe everyone is envious of you.

- You lack even the littlest of compassion towards others except at times when you want to manipulate someone, including your kids.

- You demonstrate very haughty behavior with everyone, which often grows stronger when you are around your children.

Sadly, all these character traits only take a toll on your child's sanity because being this way causes you to act and react irrationally and emotionally with your child.

How Narcissistic Parents Behave with their Kids

Narcissism makes you behave negatively with your children in the following ways:

- You constantly yell at your kids for every mistake they make, including the pettiest of things such as a 4-year-old kid spilling juice on the floor.

- You set an incredibly high criterion for your children in every aspect of their life, which, somehow, they can never fulfill because you compare their performance with yours.

- Whether it's studies, behavior, or health, you never seem too pleased with your kids. Thinking about this just reminded me of a time when I would constantly push my kids to get excellent grades, but even when they passed with flying colors, I was never happy with their results.

- You never acknowledge and appreciate your children's achievements; you always consider them very ordinary. Your kid could bring home an Olympic gold medal, and you would still have a scornful look on your face.

- You never allow your kids to speak in any matter, even if it concerns them. You never seek or take any feedback or input from them; your go-to order for them is 'shut up and follow my orders.'

- You perceive their littlest of mistakes as grim failures and constantly belittle them.

- Instead of understanding how it is human to err, you regard your kids as superhuman beings who can never falter and must always be perfect because you are comparing them to yourself.

- You never have heart-to-heart, warm chats with your kids where they can open up about their feelings.

- You prioritize your needs and wellbeing over those of your kids to the extent that you completely ignore their needs and never take their welfare into account.

- You always have a plan ready for your kids to oblige to, and never accept no as an answer from them.

- You usually ridicule your kids; you also never shy away from a chance at insulting them in front of others.

- You constantly compare your kids to other kids and remind your children of their mistakes, problems, and shortcomings.

- You deprive your kids of the love, attention, care, and appreciation they need from their parents; you always behave like a dictator with them.

Unfortunately, most narcissistic parents are unaware of how negatively such behavior influences their kids. In their opinion, such action aims to discipline and guide their kids into becoming mature, responsible, and successful grown-ups—they're trying to be "good parents."

On the contrary, your narcissistic behavior with your offspring only brings forth different problems for them.

How Narcissistic Parents Sabotage their Kids' Life

According to Ramani Durvasula and W. Keith Campbell, Psychology Professors at the University of Georgia and experts on narcissism, living with a narcissistic parent is never easy.

Imagine going home with your exam marked A+, hoping to receive a hug and warm words of admiration and encouragement from your parent only to find him/her disregarding your achievement with disdain.

Think of how you'd feel when you expected your parent to console you when you were grieving with sadness because you didn't get accepted into a college you were hoping to study in only for your mum or dad to admonish you for "not working hard enough."

Imagine how crushed you'd feel if one or both of your parents constantly told you how

-terrible a child you were, and no matter what you did, you were never good enough for your parent.

I know how painful all of this can be for a child. I know that because I went through this type of behavior with my father —I never thought I could meet his expectations of me. Regrettably, my children went through this with me.

Although I was a supportive, friendly, compassionate, and loving mother to my kids, in my attempt to be a good mother and to raise the "perfect kids," I ended up being over-bearing and over-supportive. I was always eager to make sure that my kids didn't make mistakes because it felt like their mistakes meant I had failed as a single parent.

When I look back, I can see that this desire was not healthy. It ended up denying my kids a chance to make mistakes and learn from them.

Because I was always eager to step in, especially with my firstborn son, In my quest, to have high-achieving kids for all the wrong reasons, I ended up instilling narcissistic tendencies in my kids:

Narcissism affected my children —and affects all kids— in the following, negative ways:

- They are unable to make decisions for themselves because I always directed them to behave a certain way and make certain decisions.

- They cannot clearly and effectively express their opinions to others because I never welcomed their input and feedback. I always asked them to stay quiet and follow my orders.

- -> -->> --->>> ---->>>> ----->>>>>

- They feel unfulfilled in life because I never allowed them to pursue their passions. I always forced them to focus on their academics alone.

- They have people-pleasing tendencies because they were always trying to please me, but somehow, I was never happy with their performance and success.

- They are unsure of what they want in life because I made sure they only concentrated on their studies and getting good grades.

- They don't have a strong, confident personality because I never let them explore themselves or find out who they genuinely are and wish to be. I constantly compared my kids to myself —and other 'better' kids— and wanted them to be perfect so they could erase my damaged childhood, but somehow this kept them from being comfortable in their skin.

- They have struggled with chronic stress, anxiety, and depression because they had nobody to talk with, no shoulder to cry on, and nobody with whom to discuss their problems openly. I was always busy with my issues.

All these problems have kept my kids from living a happy, meaningful, and balanced life. Fortunately, I realized how my behavior influenced my children and slowly made amends to it.

Yes, I did that very late, but I made an effort to improve my behavior with my kids as well as my relationship with them.

Now that I have embarked on this beautiful journey and am enjoying a nice, calm, and positive bond with my kids, I want you to have the same.

No parent and child should have to go through the troubles experienced by narcissistic parents and their children. I am here to facilitate you in that journey.

The following chapters guide you on how to accomplish this goal:

CHAPTER 2
STEP 1

Accept Your Problem and Understand Your Children are Individuals with Rights

To fix every problem you have ever experience in life, the first thing you need to do is acknowledge the issue. Unless you accept your issue, you can never remedy it.

This 'rule' applies to your narcissistic behavior too. To improve your bond with your kids, the first thing you need to do is accept that you have a problem.

#: Acknowledge Your Narcissistic Personality Disorder

All of us struggle with many shortcomings. While you may not consider shortcomings something to be proud of, you need to stop feeling ashamed of them as well, especially since you wish to improve on them.

Similarly, to change your narcissistic behavior so that you stop controlling and hurting your kids, accept that you have a serious problem to manage.

This acceptance helps you come to terms with your disorder and slowly assuage it so that you can stop inflicting harm on your child's personality.

- Start with consciously observing your behavior with your kids, and look for the different behavioral signs and symptoms discussed in the previous chapter.

- If you are always ridiculing, admonishing, and controlling your kids, and they are always scared of talking to you, you are a narcissistic parent.

- Sit somewhere peaceful and reflect on how your behavior influences your kids, their life, and your relationship with them. If you are honest, you will realize that the impact is only negative and feel guilty about it somewhere deep within.

- Acknowledge that guilt and accept that you have an authoritative and narcissistic personality that isn't benefitting your kids.

- Say something such as, 'I have a narcissistic personality disorder, and I am positively working towards improving it so that I can have a healthy, happy bond with my kids.' Chant this suggestion repeatedly, each time with more conviction, so that the affirmation becomes a part of your psyche and rewires you to think positively.

- Reflect on how you have emotionally abused your kids over the years and how that has affected their lives. This realization is likely to be very overwhelming; take things slow, but continue to introspect because it will help you better your behavior with them.

- -> -->> --->>> ---->>>> ----->>>>>

- Every day, commit to yourself to becoming a positive parent to your kid and recall this commitment several times during the day while consciously observing your behavior with them all along.

As you slowly work on accepting your problem, simultaneously, you need to work on embracing the fact that your kids are individuals who have individual rights. They have the right to think for themselves and make decisions, particularly if they are adults.

#: Accept Your Kids are Individuals who Have Free Will

This realization is going to be hard for you to accept, but if you take the following baby steps consciously and consistently, you will be able to start treating your kids with the respect they deserve:

- Stop giving your kids direct orders on what and how to do. If you have younger kids, provide them with the right to choose their dresses, sport to play, movie to watch, and activities to engage in —with parental supervision. If your kids are adults now, you need to stop meddling in their life. Instead of telling them what subject to majors in, ask them of their choice and approve of it. Instead of telling them what career to opt for, tell them you support their decision.

- Do not ask your children to give you a detailed report of how they spent their day; do not pass judgment on everything they do.

- If your child is not in the mood to talk to you when you are, do not force the conversation; just stick around and make sure your child knows that should he or she need someone to listen or help, you're more than glad to be that person.

- If your toddlers or slightly older kids throw a tantrum, let them do so. Do tell them not to shout publicly and throw things at you or others, but allow them to vent their frustration through tears and bickering. Doing this teaches your kids to express and accept their emotions instead of suppressing them.

- Do not check your child's phone, wallet, personal journal, and other private items as it invades their privacy —especially if you have tweens and teens.

- Stop following your child around like a helicopter-parent, saving him/her from every problem.

Slowly make these changes to your behavior so that you can give your child space to breathe and take it easy. As you work on this, you also need to start taking an interest in your children's lives and showing concern for their wellbeing.

The next chapter will show you how to do that:

Chapter 3 Step 2

Take an Interest in Your Child's Life and Be a Loving Parent

During sad times, we are often advised to fake a smile until we believe it and can feel better. That is good advice to follow as you endeavor to better your relationship with your kids and slowly make amends for all the emotional harm you have inflicted on them.

Yes, you will have to fake interest and concern for them for a while because showering affection and empathy onto others isn't something that comes naturally to narcissists. That said, if you fake it with great conviction for a while, you will eventually feel and believe it.

Here is how you need to start behaving with your children to make them feel loved and cared for:

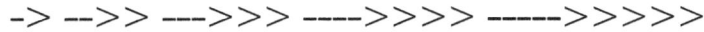

#: Greet Your Kids Happily and Encourage them to Talk

Start by greeting your kids joyously every morning and smiling at them off and on. Doing this may amaze them at first, but soon, they will get used to it and smile back at you.

At the same time, talk to them often, especially when you are together at the dinner table or running errands. Ask them of how their day was, anything they struggled with, anything they enjoyed, and about life in general.

While talking to your kids, ask them questions and give them time to answer instead of rambling on yourself. Invite their input and listen to it attentively.

Your kids may not open up at first, but if you show support and aren't too pushy, and if you continue inviting them to share their feelings and opinions, they will eventually open to you.

At this time, you need to be patient and kind to them.

#: *Stop Being Judgmental of your Kids*

When your kids share their feelings with you, even if they seem trivial to you, acknowledge them. Do not label your kids or their feelings as good, bad, positive, negative, terrible, etc.

You may not be able to show extreme empathy at first, but it's okay. If you cannot find something positive to say, don't say anything at all; sometimes, just silently sitting with your kids and listening is enough to calm them down.

Whenever your kids come to you with a problem, do not admonish them; listen to them patiently and ask for more details where you need it. Instead of reacting to their issue, take time to process it and offer advice when you have reflected on the matter.

#: Learn to Control Your Anger

Slowly work on calming your rage that is likely to come very easily and quickly whenever your kids do not oblige to your orders or do not fulfill a set criterion in a certain aspect of life.

If your 7-year-old son complains about having broccoli for dinner, control your urge to scream at him. Acknowledge that you feel frustrated, excuse yourself from the dinner table, take deep breaths, have a cool drink of water, calm yourself down, and then return to your kid.

Similarly, try to soothe your seething fury every time you find it bubbling inside you because of something your children did. As you slowly behave calmly with your kids, they will feel safer with you and find it easier to approach you when they feel worried or troubled.

#: Do Not Question their Decisions

As a narcissistic parent, it is natural to believe that you are the only authority in your house and that everyone else, especially your kids, knows nothing. This belief is why you question their choices and decisions every time.

With that said, if you want your kids to love and respect you, and to grow into confident, mature adults capable of making life-altering decisions and taking accountability for them, you need to put an end to this habit of constantly doubting their decisions.

When your 13-year-old daughter tells you that she wishes to be in the lacrosse team, not to ballet, accept and acknowledge her decisions. Force a smile, hug her, and let her know you support her.

If your 19-year-old son informs you that he wishes to go to art school instead of law school, advise him to think things through to make an informed decision, but never tell him how you think this is a bad idea.

Slowly, show your kids that you trust their decisions. After doing this for a while, your kids will start becoming more confident and comfortable in their skin. Plus, they will like you better too.

#: Praise Them Instead of Seeking Validation from Them

Additionally, make a conscious decision to praise your kids off and on for their accomplishments, strengths, personality, features, etc. If your 5-year-old kid brings you a drawing, don't say it looks crappy; instead, tell him how lovely it is. Tell your daughter how pretty she looks in her new dress, and hug your son for scoring an A in history.

You may get an urge to seek validation from them; you need to control it by showering-affection on them. You can share your stories with them, but try to cut back on the frequency.

If you work on these tips and steps consistently, you will soon start noting positive development and progress in your relationship with your kids.

As part of this book, I have included a journal meant to help you implement these strategies in your life and track your performance better:

Journal

"The best way to make children good is to make them happy."

Oscar Wilde

"Always kiss your children goodnight, even if they're already asleep."

H. Jackson Brown, Jr.

What's On My Mind?

1. _____
2. _____
3. _____

Today's Wins

1. _____
2. _____
3. _____

Today's Setbacks

1. _____
2. _____
3. _____

Highlight of the Day

"One thing I had learned from watching chimpanzees with their infants is that having a child should be fun."

Jane Goodall

Notes:

1. _____
2. _____
3. _____

""Children are apt to live up to what you believe of them."

Lady Bird Johnson

What's On My Mind?

1. _____
2. _____
3. _____

Today's Wins

1. _____
2. _____
3. _____

Today's Setbacks

1. _____
2. _____
3. _____

Highlight of the Day

"It is time for parents to teach young people that in diversity, there is beauty, and there is strength."

Maya Angelou

Notes:

1. _____
2. _____
3. _____

"My children are the reason I laugh, smile, and want to get up every morning."

Gena Lee Nolin

What's On My Mind?

1. _____
2. _____
3. _____

Today's Wins

1. _____
2. _____
3. _____

Today's Setbacks

1. _____
2. _____
3. _____

Highlight of the Day

"Having a child is like getting a tattoo ... on your face. You better be committed."

Elizabeth Gilbert

Notes:

1. _____
2. _____
3. _____

"There really are places in the heart you don't even know exist until you love a child."

Anne Lamott

What's On My Mind?

1. _____
2. _____
3. _____

Today's Wins

1. _____
2. _____
3. _____

Today's Setbacks

1. _____
2. _____
3. _____

Highlight of the Day

"Your kids require you most of all to love them for who they are, not to spend your whole time trying to correct them."

Bill Ayers

Notes:

1. _____
2. _____
3. _____

"You can learn many things from children. How much patience you have, for instance."

Franklin P. Adams

What's On My Mind?

1. _____
2. _____
3. _____

Today's Wins

1. _____
2. _____
3. _____

Today's Setbacks

1. _____
2. _____
3. _____

Highlight of the Day

"We never know the love of the parent till we become parents ourselves."

Henry Ward Beecher

Notes:

1. _____
2. _____
3. _____

"There's no way to be a perfect mother and a million ways to be a good one."

Jill Churchill

What's On My Mind?

1. _____
2. _____
3. _____

Today's Wins

1. _____
2. _____
3. _____

Today's Setbacks

1. _____
2. _____
3. _____

Highlight of the Day

"We may not be able to prepare the future for our children, but we can at least prepare our children for the future."

Franklin D. Roosevelt

Notes:

1. _____
2. _____
3. _____

"Sometimes the strength of motherhood is greater than natural laws."

Barbara Kingsolver

What's On My Mind?

1. _____
2. _____
3. _____

Today's Wins

1. _____
2. _____
3. _____

Today's Setbacks

1. _____
2. _____
3. _____

Highlight of the Day

""It just occurred to me that the majority of my diet is made up of the foods that my kid didn't finish."

Carrie Underwood

Notes:

1. _____
2. _____
3. _____

"Mother Nature is providential. She gives us twelve years to develop a love for our children before turning them into teenagers."

William Galvin

What's On My Mind?

1. _____
2. _____
3. _____

Today's Wins

1. _____
2. _____
3. _____

Today's Setbacks

1. _____
2. _____
3. _____

Highlight of the Day

"Your children are not your children, they come through you, but they are life itself, wanting to express itself."

Wayne Dyer

Notes:

1. _____
2. _____
3. _____

"I came to parenting the way most of us do — knowing nothing and trying to learn everything."

Mayim Bialik

What's On My Mind?

1. _____
2. _____
3. _____

Today's Wins

1. _____
2. _____
3. _____

Today's Setbacks

1. _____
2. _____
3. _____

Highlight of the Day

"The beauty of motherhood is in the folds and creases of our lives, the grimaces and tantrums, the moments when we have to grit our teeth to get through."

Robyn Passante

Notes:

1. _____
2. _____
3. _____

"Parenting without a sense of humor is like being an accountant who sucks at math."

Amber Dusick

What's On My Mind?

1. _____
2. _____
3. _____

Today's Wins

1. _____
2. _____
3. _____

Today's Setbacks

1. _____
2. _____
3. _____

Highlight of the Day

"Behind every young child who believes in himself is a parent who believed first."

Matthew Jacobson

Notes:

1. _____
2. _____
3. _____

"The way we talk to our children becomes their inner voice."

Peggy O'Mara

What's On My Mind?

1. _____
2. _____
3. _____

Today's Wins

1. _____
2. _____
3. _____

Today's Setbacks

1. _____
2. _____
3. _____

Highlight of the Day

"The thing about parenting rules is there aren't any. That's what makes it so difficult."

Ewan McGregor

Notes:

1. _____
2. _____
3. _____

"Being a mother is learning about strengths you didn't know you had, and dealing with fears you didn't know existed."

Linda Wooten

What's On My Mind?

1. _____
2. _____
3. _____

Today's Wins

1. _____
2. _____
3. _____

Today's Setbacks

1. _____
2. _____
3. _____

Highlight of the Day

"If you bungle raising your children, I don't think whatever else you do matters very much."

Jackie Kennedy

Notes:

1. _____
2. _____
3. _____

"To raise a child, it sometimes takes a village...but sometimes that village should shut up and mind their own business."

Susan McLean

What's On My Mind?
1. _____
2. _____
3. _____

Today's Wins
1. _____
2. _____
3. _____

Today's Setbacks
1. _____
2. _____
3. _____

Highlight of the Day

"Parenthood...it's about guiding the next generation and forgiving the last."

Peter Krause

Notes:
1. _____
2. _____
3. _____

"Your kids require you most of all to love them for who they are, not to spend your whole time trying to correct them."

Bill Ayers

What's On My Mind?

1. _____
2. _____
3. _____

Today's Wins

1. _____
2. _____
3. _____

Today's Setbacks

1. _____
2. _____
3. _____

Highlight of the Day

"To be in your children's memories tomorrow, You have to be in their lives today."

Barbara Johnson

Notes:

1. _____
2. _____
3. _____

"Children have never been very good at listening to their elders, but they have never failed to imitate them."

James Baldwin

What's On My Mind?

1. _____
2. _____
3. _____

Today's Wins

1. _____
2. _____
3. _____

Today's Setbacks

1. _____
2. _____
3. _____

Highlight of the Day

"Parenting is one of the best management training programs there is."

Irene Rosenfeld

Notes:

1. _____
2. _____
3. _____

"Your kids require you most of all to love them for who they are, not to spend your whole time trying to correct them."

Bill Ayers

What's On My Mind?

1. _____
2. _____
3. _____

Today's Wins

1. _____
2. _____
3. _____

Today's Setbacks

1. _____
2. _____
3. _____

Highlight of the Day

"To be in your children's memories tomorrow, You have to be in their lives today."

Barbara Johnson

Notes:

1. _____
2. _____
3. _____

Free Writing Area

"Journaling is like whispering to one's self and listening at the same time."

Mina Murray

Free Writing Area

Free Writing Area

FREE WRITING AREA

Free Writing Area

Free Writing Area

Free Writing Area

Free Writing Area

Free Writing Area

Free Writing Area

Free Writing Area

FREE WRITING AREA

Free Writing Area

Free Writing Area

Free Writing Area

Free Writing Area

Free Writing Area

Free Writing Area

Free Writing Area

Free Writing Area

Free Writing Area

Free Writing Area

Free Writing Area

Free Writing Area

Free Writing Area

Free Writing Area

Free Writing Area

Free Writing Area

Free Writing Area

Free Writing Area

Free Writing Area

Free Writing Area

Free Writing Area

Free Writing Area

FREE WRITING AREA

Free Writing Area

Free Writing Area

Free Writing Area

Free Writing Area

Free Writing Area

Free Writing Area

Free Writing Area

Free Writing Area

Free Writing Area

Free Writing Area

Free Writing Area

Free Writing Area

Free Writing Area

Free Writing Area

Free Writing Area

Free Writing Area

Free Writing Area

FREE WRITING AREA

Free Writing Area

Free Writing Area

Free Writing Area

Free Writing Area

Free Writing Area

Free Writing Area

FREE WRITING AREA

Free Writing Area

FREE WRITING AREA

Free Writing Area

Free Writing Area

Free Writing Area

Free Writing Area

Free Writing Area

Free Writing Area

Free Writing Area

Free Writing Area

Free Writing Area

Free Writing Area

Free Writing Area

Free Writing Area

Free Writing Area

Free Writing Area

Free Writing Area

Free Writing Area

FREE WRITING AREA

Free Writing Area

FREE WRITING AREA

Free Writing Area

Free Writing Area

Free Writing Area

Free Writing Area

Free Writing Area

Free Writing Area

Free Writing Area

Free Writing Area

Free Writing Area

FREE WRITING AREA

Free Writing Area

Free Writing Area

Free Writing Area

Free Writing Area

Free Writing Area

Free Writing Area

Free Writing Area

Free Writing Area

Free Writing Area

FREE WRITING AREA

Free Writing Area

Free Writing Area

Free Writing Area

Free Writing Area

Free Writing Area

Free Writing Area

Free Writing Area

Free Writing Area

Free Writing Area

Free Writing Area

Free Writing Area

Free Writing Area

Free Writing Area

Free Writing Area

Free Writing Area

Free Writing Area

Free Writing Area

Free Writing Area

Free Writing Area

Free Writing Area

Free Writing Area

Free Writing Area

FREE WRITING AREA

Free Writing Area

Free Writing Area

Free Writing Area

Free Writing Area

FREE WRITING AREA

Free Writing Area

Free Writing Area

Free Writing Area

Free Writing Area

FREE WRITING AREA

Free Writing Area

Free Writing Area

Free Writing Area

Free Writing Area

Conclusion

I sincerely hope this book gave you real value, and that it helps you create a positive relationship with your kids to ensure that they don't become narcissistic adults.

© Patrice M Foster

Learn More About Patrice M Foster From:

https://patricemfoster.com
https://patricemdepressioncourses.com/

www.ingramcontent.com/pod-product-compliance
Lightning Source LLC
LaVergne TN
LVHW041618070426
835507LV00008B/316